Millennial Money Mastery The Ultimate Guide to Financial Success

Jakinson

Millennial Money Mastery The Ultimate Guide to Financial Success

Copyright © 2023 by Jakinson

This book is a work of fiction. Names, characters, places, and incidents either are the product of the author's imagination or are used fictitiously. Any resemblance to actual events, locales, persons, living or dead, is entirely coincidental.

The first edition was published in 2023

ISBN:

Published by:
Noya
1663 Liberty Drive
Hyderabad, IN 47403
www.noyapublishers.com

This book is self-published using on-demand printing and publishing, which allows it to be printed and distributed globally.

TABLE OF CONTENTS

Chapter 8: Creating a Wealth Mindset and Long-Term Financial Success 68

Conclusion: Embracing Financial Independence as a Millennial 78

Chapter 1: Understanding Financial Success for Millennials

The Importance of Financial Literacy

In today's fast-paced and ever-changing world, financial literacy has become more crucial than ever, especially for millennials. As young adults, we strive to achieve financial success and security, but often find ourselves ill-equipped to navigate the complex world of personal finance. This subchapter aims to shed light on the importance of financial literacy and its role in helping millennials achieve their financial goals.

First and foremost, financial literacy empowers individuals to make informed and responsible financial decisions. Understanding concepts such as budgeting, investing, and debt management allows millennials to take control of their financial future. By acquiring the necessary knowledge and skills, we can avoid common pitfalls and make choices that align with our long-term goals.

Furthermore, financial literacy provides a solid foundation for cultivating good financial habits. It enables us to develop a clear understanding of our financial situation, including income, expenses, and savings. Armed with this knowledge, we can create realistic budgets, track our spending, and establish saving goals. These habits not only help us achieve short-term financial stability but also lay the groundwork for long-term financial success.

Additionally, financial literacy equips millennials with the tools to navigate the increasingly complex financial landscape. From student loans and credit cards to mortgages and retirement planning, the financial decisions we face can be overwhelming. However, with a strong understanding of financial concepts and principles, we can confidently navigate these challenges and make choices that align with our values and aspirations.

Moreover, financial literacy plays a vital role in building resilience and overcoming financial setbacks. Life is unpredictable, and unexpected emergencies or financial hardships can occur at any time. With a solid understanding of personal finance, we can develop emergency funds, insurance plans, and contingency strategies. This preparedness enables us to weather financial storms and bounce back stronger.

In conclusion, financial literacy is a fundamental component of achieving financial success as millennials. By acquiring knowledge and skills in personal finance, we can make informed decisions, cultivate good financial habits, navigate the complexities of the financial landscape, and build resilience against unexpected setbacks. "Millennial Money Mastery: The Ultimate Guide to Financial Success" aims to empower millennials with the necessary tools and knowledge to master their finances and achieve their goals.

The Millennial Financial Landscape

As millennials, we find ourselves navigating a unique financial landscape, filled with both opportunities and challenges. In this subchapter, we will delve into some of the key factors that shape our generation's financial journey, and provide the ultimate guide to achieving financial success in this ever-evolving world.

One of the defining characteristics of the millennial financial landscape is the increasing burden of student loan debt. Many of us have pursued higher education to secure better career prospects, but this investment often comes with a hefty price tag. We will explore strategies to effectively manage student loans, including refinancing options, loan forgiveness programs, and smart repayment strategies.

Additionally, the rise of the gig economy has presented millennials with new opportunities for income generation. We will discuss the advantages and disadvantages of gig work, and provide tips on how to maximize earnings in this flexible job market. From leveraging online platforms to exploring freelance opportunities, we will guide you towards financial stability and success in this ever-evolving gig economy.

While technology has undoubtedly transformed our lives, it has also revolutionized the way we handle our finances. From mobile banking to robo-advisors, we have access to a myriad of digital tools that can aid us in our financial journey. We will explore these technological advancements and provide insights on how to leverage them to boost savings, manage investments, and track spending habits.

Furthermore, the millennial financial landscape is heavily influenced by our unique attitudes and values. We prioritize experiences over material possessions, and are conscious of the impact our purchasing decisions have on the environment and society. In this subchapter, we will delve into sustainable investing, ethical consumerism, and responsible spending, empowering you to align your financial goals with your values.

Lastly, we will address the importance of financial literacy in this complex landscape. Many millennials have not received adequate education on personal finance, leading to financial pitfalls and missed opportunities. We will provide a comprehensive guide to understanding credit scores, building a budget, investing in stocks and real estate, and planning for retirement.

In conclusion, the millennial financial landscape is a dynamic and ever-changing environment. By understanding the unique challenges and opportunities it presents, and equipping ourselves with the necessary knowledge and tools, we can confidently navigate this landscape and achieve the ultimate financial success.

Setting Financial Goals

In the pursuit of financial success, one of the most crucial steps for millennials is setting clear and achievable financial goals. Without a well-defined target, it can be challenging to stay motivated and make progress towards financial independence. This subchapter will guide you through the process of setting effective financial goals that align with your personal values and aspirations.

1. Understand Your Why: Before diving into the nitty-gritty of goal setting, take a moment to reflect on your values and long-term aspirations. What does financial success mean to you? Is it owning a home, starting your own business, or traveling the world? Understanding your "why" will provide the necessary motivation and direction to set meaningful financial goals.

2. Set SMART Goals: To ensure your goals are effective and attainable, apply the SMART framework. SMART stands for Specific, Measurable, Achievable, Relevant, and Time-bound. For example, instead of setting a vague goal like "save more money," a SMART goal would be "save $10,000 for a down payment on a house in the next two years." This specific and time-bound goal allows you to track progress and make necessary adjustments along the way.

3. Prioritize: As millennials, you may have numerous financial objectives, such as paying off student loans, saving for retirement, or starting a family. It is crucial to prioritize your goals based on their importance and urgency. Focus on one or two primary objectives at a time to avoid spreading yourself too thin and losing focus.

4. Break It Down: Large financial goals can be overwhelming and challenging to achieve without a clear plan. Break down your long-term goals into smaller, manageable milestones. For instance, if your goal is to pay off $50,000 in student loans within five years, break it down into monthly or annual targets. This approach allows you to celebrate small wins along the way and stay motivated.

5. Review and Adjust: Periodically review your financial goals to ensure they are still aligned with your values and aspirations. Life circumstances change, and your goals should adapt accordingly. Make adjustments as needed, whether it's increasing or decreasing the target amount or modifying the timeline. Flexibility is key to staying on track and maintaining motivation.

By following these steps, you will be well on your way to mastering your finances and achieving long-term financial success. Remember, setting goals is only the first step—the real work lies in taking consistent action and staying committed to your objectives. With determination and perseverance, you can create a solid foundation for your financial future.

Chapter 2: Building a Strong Financial Foundation

Managing Debt and Student Loans

In this digital age, where financial responsibilities are constantly evolving, it is crucial for millennials to master the art of managing debt and student loans. The burden of student loans can be overwhelming, but with the right strategies, you can pave your way to financial success. This subchapter of "Millennial Money Mastery: The Ultimate Guide to Financial Success" aims to provide you with practical tips and insights on effectively managing your debt and student loans.

Firstly, it is essential to have a clear understanding of your debt. Take the time to gather all relevant information about your loans, including interest rates, repayment terms, and any additional fees. This knowledge will empower you to make informed decisions and devise a proactive plan to tackle your debt.

One of the most effective strategies for managing debt is creating a budget. By carefully tracking your income and expenses, you can identify areas where you can cut back and allocate more funds towards debt repayment. Prioritize your debt payments by targeting high-interest loans first, as this will save you money in the long run.

Consider exploring loan consolidation or refinancing options. Consolidating multiple loans into one can simplify your repayment process and potentially lower your interest rates. Refinancing, on the other hand, allows you to negotiate new terms and rates, which can significantly reduce your monthly payments.

Don't be afraid to seek professional assistance. Financial advisors or credit counseling agencies can provide expert guidance on debt management strategies tailored to your specific situation. They can help negotiate with lenders, establish manageable payment plans, and even provide valuable tips on improving your credit score.

Additionally, leverage any available resources to aid in your debt repayment journey. Explore loan forgiveness programs, scholarships, or employer-sponsored assistance programs. These opportunities can alleviate your financial burden and accelerate your path to debt freedom.

While managing debt is crucial, don't forget to invest in your financial future. Set aside a portion of your income for savings and investments. Building an emergency fund will provide you with a safety net during unexpected situations and prevent you from falling into further debt.

In conclusion, mastering the art of managing debt and student loans is a crucial step towards achieving financial success as a millennial. By understanding your debt, creating a budget, exploring consolidation options, seeking professional advice, and leveraging available resources, you can effectively tackle your debt and pave the way for a brighter financial future. Remember, it is never too late to take control of your financial situation and work towards a debt-free life.

Creating a Budget that Works for You

In today's fast-paced world, financial success is something that every millennial strives for. However, achieving this goal can be challenging without a well-planned budget. A budget is an essential tool that helps you take control of your finances and make informed decisions about your spending. In this subchapter, we will explore the key steps to creating a budget that works for you, guiding you towards ultimate financial success.

1. Assess your financial goals: Begin by identifying your short-term and long-term financial goals. Whether it's saving for a down payment on a house, paying off student loans, or traveling the world, understanding your objectives will provide you with the motivation to stick to your budget.

2. Track your income and expenses: To create an effective budget, you must have a clear understanding of your income and expenses. Start by listing all your sources of income, including your salary, side hustles, or passive income. Then, track your monthly expenses, categorizing them into essential (rent, groceries, utilities) and non-essential (entertainment, dining out). This will give you a comprehensive overview of your financial situation.

3. Set realistic spending limits: Once you have a clear picture of your income and expenses, it's time to set realistic spending limits for each category. Allocate a portion of your income towards savings and debt repayment, ensuring that your essential expenses are covered. Be mindful of your non-essential spending and make adjustments to align with your financial goals.

4. Embrace the 50/30/20 rule: A popular budgeting rule for millennials is the 50/30/20 rule. This rule recommends allocating 50% of your income towards essential expenses, 30% towards non-essential expenses, and 20% towards

savings and debt repayment. Adhering to this guideline ensures that you strike a balance between enjoying your present and securing your future.

5. Regularly review and adjust your budget: Your budget should not be set in stone. As your financial situation evolves, it's important to regularly review and adjust your budget accordingly. Life events such as a raise, a new job, or unexpected expenses may require modifications to your spending limits. Stay flexible and make changes as needed to ensure your budget remains effective.

Creating a budget that works for you is a crucial step towards achieving financial success as a millennial. By assessing your financial goals, tracking your income and expenses, setting realistic spending limits, embracing the 50/30/20 rule, and regularly reviewing your budget, you will be on your way to ultimate financial success. Remember, a well-planned budget is not restrictive but rather empowering, providing you with the freedom to make informed financial decisions and live the life you desire.

Building an Emergency Fund

In today's unpredictable world, having a solid financial foundation is more important than ever. As millennials, we face unique challenges when it comes to achieving financial success. From student loan debt to a volatile job market, it can feel overwhelming to think about our financial future. However, one essential step towards financial security is building an emergency fund.

An emergency fund is a pot of money set aside specifically for unexpected expenses or financial emergencies. It acts as a safety net, providing peace of mind and a sense of security. Whether it's a medical emergency, a car repair, or a sudden job loss, having an emergency fund can help you navigate these unexpected situations without derailing your financial goals.

So, how do you go about building an emergency fund? Here are some key steps to get you started on the path to financial stability:

1. Set a Savings Goal: Determine how much you want to save in your emergency fund. A good rule of thumb is to aim for at least three to six months of living expenses. This will give you a buffer in case of any unexpected setbacks.

2. Track Your Expenses: Take a close look at your monthly expenses and identify areas where you can cut back. By making small adjustments, you can redirect more money towards your emergency fund.

3. Create a Budget: Establish a budget that prioritizes saving. Allocate a portion of your income specifically towards your emergency fund. Treat it as a non-negotiable expense, just like paying rent or utilities.

4. Automate Your Savings: Set up an automatic transfer from your checking account to your emergency fund. This

way, you won't even have to think about saving – it will happen effortlessly.

5. Avoid Temptation: Stay focused on your long-term financial goals and resist the urge to dip into your emergency fund for non-emergency purposes. Remember, the fund is there to provide you with financial security and peace of mind.

Building an emergency fund is a crucial step in achieving financial success. By taking proactive measures to save for unexpected expenses, you'll gain a sense of control over your finances and be better prepared for whatever life throws your way. Start today, and let your emergency fund be your financial safety net.

Establishing Credit and Managing Credit Cards

Subchapter: Establishing Credit and Managing Credit Cards

Introduction:
In today's fast-paced world, financial success is a key priority for millennials. To achieve this, it is essential to understand the importance of establishing credit and managing credit cards effectively. This subchapter aims to guide young adults through the process of building creditworthiness and making smart choices with credit cards, ultimately empowering them to achieve their financial goals.

Building   Credit:
Establishing credit is the foundation of financial success. It enables millennials to access loans, secure favorable interest rates, and make significant purchases such as a home or car. To begin building credit, it is crucial to open a credit card or take out a small loan. Start by obtaining a secured credit card, which requires a deposit as collateral, or seek credit-building products tailored to millennials. Consistently making on-time payments and keeping credit utilization low will gradually improve credit scores.

Managing   Credit   Cards:
Credit cards can be powerful tools if managed wisely. Unfortunately, misusing them can lead to financial distress. To avoid unnecessary debt and maximize the benefits of credit cards, millennials should follow these key principles:

1. Choose the right credit card: Research and compare credit card options to find one that aligns with your spending habits and offers rewards or cashback programs. Look for low or no annual fees and competitive interest rates.

2. Establish a budget: Create a monthly budget and stick to it. Ensure you have enough income to cover your expenses and credit card payments. Avoid overspending and accumulating debt beyond your means.

3. Pay your balance in full: Aim to pay off your credit card balance in full each month. If you cannot, pay more than the minimum payment to reduce interest charges. Carrying a balance can lead to long-term debt and financial stress.

4. Track your spending: Regularly review your credit card statements to identify any fraudulent or unauthorized charges. This practice also helps you understand your spending patterns and make necessary adjustments.

5. Avoid unnecessary debt: Use credit cards for essential purchases and emergencies only. Avoid making impulsive or unnecessary purchases that can lead to unnecessary debt.

Conclusion:
Establishing credit and managing credit cards are vital aspects of millennial financial success. By building credit responsibly and using credit cards wisely, millennials can pave the way to favorable interest rates, financial independence, and achieving their long-term goals. Remember, financial success is not just about earning money but also about managing it effectively. By implementing these strategies, millennials can take control of their financial future and build a solid foundation for a prosperous life.

Chapter 3: Saving and Investing Strategies for Millennials

The Power of Saving

In this fast-paced world of instant gratification, it's easy for millennials to get caught up in the cycle of spending without considering the long-term consequences. However, the power of saving cannot be underestimated when it comes to achieving financial success. In this subchapter, we will explore the various ways in which saving can transform your financial future and provide you with the ultimate guide to financial success.

First and foremost, saving allows you to build a solid financial foundation. By setting aside a portion of your income regularly, you create a safety net for unexpected expenses and emergencies. This not only gives you peace of mind but also prevents you from relying on credit cards or loans, which can lead to a never-ending cycle of debt.

Saving also enables you to pursue your dreams and goals. Whether it's buying a house, starting a business, or traveling the world, having a savings account specifically designated for your aspirations can make them a reality. By consistently saving, you are taking control of your financial destiny and giving yourself the freedom to pursue the things that truly matter to you.

Moreover, saving allows you to take advantage of investment opportunities. By accumulating a substantial amount of savings, you can explore various investment options such as stocks, real estate, or mutual funds. Investments have the potential to generate passive income and grow your wealth over time, paving the way for long-term financial success.

Additionally, saving instills discipline and financial responsibility. It teaches you to prioritize your needs over wants and make conscious decisions about your spending habits. By practicing delayed gratification and resisting unnecessary purchases, you develop a sense of self-control that will benefit you not only in your financial journey but also in other aspects of your life.

Lastly, saving builds financial independence. As a millennial, being financially independent means having the freedom to make choices that align with your values and goals, without being burdened by financial constraints. Saving provides the necessary resources to achieve this independence and create a life of financial abundance and security.

In conclusion, the power of saving cannot be overstated in the journey towards financial success. By prioritizing saving, you can build a solid foundation, pursue your dreams, take advantage of investment opportunities, develop discipline, and ultimately achieve financial independence. So, start harnessing the power of saving today and pave the way for a brighter financial future.

Types of Savings Accounts and Their Benefits

In this subchapter, we will explore the various types of savings accounts available to millennials and discuss their unique benefits. As millennials, we understand the importance of saving money and building a strong financial foundation for a successful future. By choosing the right savings account, we can maximize our savings potential and achieve our financial goals.

1. Basic Savings Account: This is the most common type of savings account offered by banks and financial institutions. It provides a safe place to store your money while earning a modest interest rate. Basic savings accounts are ideal for emergency funds or short-term savings goals.

2. High-Yield Savings Account: For millennials looking to grow their savings at a faster rate, a high-yield savings account is a great option. These accounts offer higher interest rates than basic savings accounts, allowing your money to work harder for you. High-yield savings accounts are suitable for long-term savings goals and can help you accumulate wealth over time.

3. Money Market Account: A money market account combines the benefits of a savings account and a checking account. It typically offers higher interest rates than basic savings accounts and allows limited check-writing abilities. Money market accounts are great for millennials who want easy access to their savings while still earning a competitive interest rate.

4. Certificates of Deposit (CDs): CDs are time-based savings accounts that offer a fixed interest rate for a specified period, ranging from a few months to several years. They are ideal for millennials with

long-term savings goals and a willingness to lock their money away for a specific duration. CDs often have higher interest rates than regular savings accounts, making them an attractive option for those seeking guaranteed returns.

5.   Retirement   Savings   Accounts: As millennials, it's never too early to start planning for retirement. Retirement savings accounts, such as 401(k) and Individual Retirement Accounts (IRAs), offer tax advantages and long-term growth potential. By contributing to these accounts, we can take advantage of employer matching contributions and compound interest, ensuring a comfortable retirement in the future.

Choosing the right savings account depends on your financial goals and risk tolerance. Consider the interest rates, fees, accessibility, and flexibility of each account before making a decision. Remember, it's essential to regularly review and reassess your savings strategy as your financial situation evolves.

By understanding the different types of savings accounts available and their benefits, millennials can make informed decisions to secure their financial success. Start saving today and take control of your financial future.

Introduction to Investing

Investing is a critical component of achieving financial success, and as millennials, it is crucial for us to understand and harness the power of investing to secure our financial future. In this subchapter, we will delve into the basics of investing, providing you with the knowledge and tools necessary to make informed investment decisions.

In today's fast-paced and ever-changing world, traditional methods of saving and relying solely on a paycheck are no longer sufficient. Investing offers the opportunity to grow our wealth by putting our hard-earned money to work. Whether you are saving for retirement, planning to start a business, or simply seeking to increase your net worth, investing is the key to realizing your financial goals.

But where do we start? Investing can be intimidating, especially if you have little to no prior knowledge. Fear not, as this subchapter will break down the fundamental concepts and strategies of investing, making it accessible and understandable for millennials like us.

We will begin by exploring the various investment vehicles available, such as stocks, bonds, mutual funds, and real estate. Each investment option carries its own set of risks and returns, and it is vital to understand these differences to make informed decisions. We will discuss the importance of diversification, asset allocation, and risk management, helping you build a well-rounded investment portfolio.

Moreover, we will delve into the mindset and psychology behind successful investing. Emotions often play a significant role in investment decisions, and understanding how to navigate this aspect is crucial. We will address common cognitive biases and provide strategies to overcome them, ensuring that your investment decisions are based on rational thinking rather than impulsive emotions.

Additionally, this subchapter will introduce you to various investment strategies, such as long-term investing, value investing, and index fund investing. We will discuss the pros and cons of each approach, helping you identify the strategy that aligns with your financial goals and risk tolerance.

By the end of this subchapter, you will have a solid foundation in investing, empowering you to make informed decisions that will set you on the path to financial success. Remember, investing is a journey, and continuous learning and adaptation are essential. So, let's dive in and unlock the world of investing together!

Understanding Different Investment Options

Investing is a crucial aspect of achieving financial success in today's world. As millennials, we have unique opportunities and challenges when it comes to investing our hard-earned money. This subchapter aims to provide you with a comprehensive understanding of different investment options available to us, enabling you to make informed decisions and secure your financial future.

1. Stocks and Bonds: Stocks represent ownership in a company, while bonds are debt securities. Both options offer potential returns and risks. Investing in stocks can provide long-term growth potential, but it comes with greater volatility. On the other hand, bonds offer fixed interest payments and are considered safer. Understanding the dynamics of these investments can help you create a balanced portfolio.

2. Mutual Funds and Exchange-Traded Funds (ETFs): Mutual funds and ETFs pool money from multiple investors to invest in diversified portfolios of stocks, bonds, or other assets. These investments offer instant diversification and are managed by professionals. Mutual funds are actively managed, while ETFs are passively managed. Researching the fees, historical performance, and investment strategy of these funds is crucial before making any investment decisions.

3. Real Estate: Real estate offers both income and potential appreciation. Investing in properties, whether residential or commercial, can provide a steady stream of rental income and long-term capital appreciation. Additionally, real estate investment trusts (REITs) allow you to invest in real estate without directly owning properties. Understanding the market,

property management, and financing options is essential for successful real estate investments.

4. Retirement Accounts: Millennials should take advantage of retirement accounts such as 401(k) plans or individual retirement accounts (IRAs). These tax-advantaged accounts allow you to invest in a variety of assets, and your contributions may be tax-deductible or tax-free. Understanding the contribution limits, employer matching, and investment choices within these accounts is crucial for maximizing your retirement savings.

5. Alternative Investments: Alternative investments include commodities, precious metals, cryptocurrencies, and peer-to-peer lending. These investments provide diversification beyond traditional assets. However, they can be riskier and require a deeper understanding of the underlying markets.

Remember, investing is a long-term game. It's essential to set clear financial goals, understand your risk tolerance, and diversify your investments to manage risk effectively. Continuously educating yourself about different investment options and seeking professional advice when needed will help you navigate the complex world of investing and achieve financial success.

In conclusion, by grasping the basics of different investment options, you can make informed decisions that align with your financial goals. The key to financial success lies in understanding the risks, rewards, and potential pitfalls associated with each investment option. With this knowledge, you can confidently navigate the investment landscape and create a strong foundation for your financial future.

Creating a Diversified Investment Portfolio

In the fast-paced world of finance, millennials are increasingly recognizing the importance of creating a diversified investment portfolio. As the generation burdened with student loans and a volatile job market, millennials are seeking ways to secure their financial future and achieve long-term success. This subchapter aims to provide millennials with a comprehensive guide to building a diversified investment portfolio, ultimately leading them towards financial success.

Diversification is a vital strategy for minimizing risk and increasing the potential for higher returns. By spreading investments across different asset classes, such as stocks, bonds, real estate, and alternative investments, millennials can reduce the impact of market fluctuations on their overall portfolio. This subchapter will not only delve into the different types of investments but also provide insights on how to allocate assets based on risk tolerance, time horizon, and financial goals.

One key aspect of creating a diversified investment portfolio is understanding the concept of risk and reward. Millennials need to balance their desire for higher returns with the need to protect their capital. This subchapter will explore various risk profiles and investment strategies suitable for different risk appetites, helping millennials make informed decisions based on their individual circumstances.

Additionally, this subchapter will shed light on the importance of regularly reviewing and rebalancing a portfolio. As millennials progress in their careers and experience life changes, their investment needs and goals may evolve. By periodically reassessing their portfolio and making necessary adjustments, millennials can ensure that their investments remain aligned with their financial objectives.

Furthermore, this subchapter will address the potential benefits of investing in socially responsible companies. With millennials being more socially and environmentally conscious than previous generations, impact investing has gained significant popularity. By incorporating investments that align with their values, millennials can achieve financial success while making a positive impact on society.

Ultimately, by creating a diversified investment portfolio, millennials can position themselves for long-term financial success. This subchapter will equip readers with the knowledge and tools necessary to navigate the complexities of investing, empowering them to make sound financial decisions and achieve their financial goals. Whether they are just starting their investment journey or looking to optimize their existing portfolio, this subchapter will serve as the ultimate guide to financial success for millennials.

Chapter 4: Building Multiple Streams of Income

The Gig Economy: Leveraging Side Hustles

In today's fast-paced and ever-changing world, millennials are constantly seeking ways to maximize their earning potential and secure financial success. This desire for financial independence has led many millennials to embrace the gig economy and leverage the power of side hustles. In this subchapter, we will delve into the gig economy and explore how millennials can effectively leverage side hustles to achieve their financial goals.

The gig economy, characterized by temporary and flexible jobs, has revolutionized the way people work and earn money. Unlike traditional nine-to-five jobs, gig work offers millennials the freedom to choose when, where, and how they work. With the rise of platforms like Uber, Airbnb, and Upwork, millennials now have an array of options to tap into their skills and talents to generate additional income.

Leveraging side hustles can be a game-changer for millennials on their journey to financial success. Not only does it provide an opportunity to increase income, but it also allows for personal and professional growth. Side hustles give millennials the chance to explore their passions, develop new skills, and build a diverse network of contacts.

To effectively leverage side hustles, millennials must first identify their strengths and interests. What skills do they possess that can be monetized? Are there any hobbies or talents that can be turned into profitable ventures? By answering these questions, millennials can discover side hustles that align with their passions, ensuring they enjoy the work they are doing.

Once a side hustle is chosen, it is crucial to create a solid plan and set clear goals. This includes determining how many hours can be dedicated to the side hustle, setting achievable income targets, and creating a marketing strategy to attract clients or customers. Millennials should also consider the financial implications of their side hustle, such as taxes and expenses, to ensure they are maximizing their earnings.

Moreover, millennials should not underestimate the importance of time management and work-life balance when juggling a side hustle alongside their primary job or studies. While side hustles offer flexibility, effective time management is essential to prevent burnout and maintain productivity.

In conclusion, the gig economy presents millennials with a unique opportunity to leverage side hustles and achieve financial success. By identifying their strengths, setting goals, and managing their time effectively, millennials can tap into the power of side hustles to increase their income, gain valuable experience, and ultimately attain financial independence.

Exploring Passive Income Opportunities

In today's fast-paced world, millennials are constantly seeking ways to achieve financial success and create a secure future. With the rising cost of living and the desire for financial freedom, it's no wonder that passive income has become a hot topic among this generation. This subchapter will delve into the various passive income opportunities available to millennials, providing them with an ultimate guide to financial success.

Passive income refers to money earned with little to no effort on your part. It's the dream of making money while you sleep or go on vacation – a concept that has become increasingly popular with the millennial generation. By exploring passive income opportunities, millennials can break free from the traditional 9-to-5 grind and build a stream of income that works for them.

One key opportunity for generating passive income is through real estate investments. From rental properties to real estate crowdfunding platforms, millennials have a range of options to explore. We will discuss the pros and cons of each, providing guidance on how to get started and make smart investment decisions in the real estate market.

Another avenue to explore is the world of online entrepreneurship. With the rise of e-commerce, social media, and digital marketing, millennials have a unique advantage in building online businesses. We will delve into the different online business models, such as affiliate marketing, dropshipping, and creating digital products, providing step-by-step guidance on how to start and grow a successful online venture.

Additionally, this subchapter will explore the power of passive investing. Millennials can learn about index funds, robo-advisors, and other investment vehicles that require minimal effort and offer the potential for long-term financial growth. We will provide insights on diversifying investment portfolios and maximizing returns without spending hours analyzing the stock market.

Lastly, we will discuss the importance of building passive income streams that align with millennials' passions and interests. By leveraging their skills and hobbies, millennials can turn their passions into profitable ventures. We will provide practical tips on monetizing creative pursuits, such as blogging, podcasting, and YouTube channels.

In conclusion, exploring passive income opportunities is a crucial step towards achieving financial success for millennials. By understanding the various avenues available, millennials can create a diversified income portfolio that generates money even when they're not actively working. This subchapter will serve as the ultimate guide, equipping millennials with the knowledge and tools they need to embark on their journey towards financial freedom.

Investing in Real Estate for Millennials

As millennials, we are often bombarded with conflicting advice about how to secure our financial future. With so many options available, it can be overwhelming to decide where to invest our hard-earned money. However, one avenue that holds great potential for long-term financial success is real estate investment.

Real estate has long been considered a stable and lucrative investment, and millennials should not overlook its advantages. In this subchapter, we will explore why real estate is an excellent investment opportunity for our generation and how we can navigate the market to maximize our returns.

First and foremost, real estate provides a tangible asset that can appreciate over time. Unlike stocks or mutual funds, which can be volatile and unpredictable, real estate tends to hold its value and even increase in worth over the years. By investing in real estate early in our lives, we can take advantage of the power of compound interest and build significant wealth over time.

Moreover, real estate offers opportunities for passive income through rental properties. Many millennials are embracing the gig economy and side hustles, but owning rental properties provides a consistent and reliable source of income. With the rise of platforms like Airbnb, it has become easier than ever to generate income from real estate investments.

However, investing in real estate requires careful planning and research. In this subchapter, we will provide a step-by-step guide to help millennials navigate the real estate market successfully. We will cover topics such as saving for a down payment, understanding mortgage options, and finding the right property in the right location.

Additionally, we will explore alternative real estate investment options, such as real estate investment trusts (REITs) and crowdfunding platforms. These options allow millennials to invest in real estate without the need for substantial capital or the hassle of property management.

In conclusion, investing in real estate can be a game-changer for millennials seeking financial success. By understanding the benefits and potential pitfalls of real estate investment, we can make informed decisions and secure our financial future. This subchapter will equip millennials with the knowledge and tools they need to embark on their real estate investment journey confidently.

Starting and Growing a Successful Online Business

In today's digital age, starting and growing a successful online business has become an increasingly popular and viable option for millennials seeking financial success. With the power of the internet at our fingertips, the opportunities are endless, and the potential for creating a thriving online business is truly within reach.

One of the key advantages of starting an online business is the low barrier to entry. Unlike traditional brick-and-mortar businesses, an online business requires minimal upfront investment and overhead costs. This makes it accessible to millennials who may have limited funds but possess a wealth of creativity and innovative ideas.

To embark on this journey, first, identify your niche. What are you passionate about? What skills or knowledge do you possess that can be monetized? By focusing on a niche market, you can position yourself as an expert and stand out from the competition. Conduct thorough market research to understand your target audience and their needs, allowing you to tailor your products or services accordingly.

Building a strong online presence is crucial for success. Create a professional website that showcases your offerings and provides a seamless user experience. Utilize social media platforms to connect with your target audience, share valuable content, and build a community around your brand. Implement effective search engine optimization strategies to increase your visibility and attract organic traffic to your website.

Furthermore, establish a robust marketing and branding strategy. Develop a unique selling proposition that differentiates your business from competitors. Leverage digital marketing techniques such as email marketing, content marketing, and influencer partnerships to reach a wider audience and drive conversions. Consistently monitor and analyze your marketing efforts to optimize your strategies and achieve maximum results.

Another essential aspect of growing a successful online business is customer satisfaction. Provide exceptional customer service and prioritize building long-term relationships with your customers. Encourage feedback and implement improvements based on their suggestions. By delivering a superior customer experience, you will foster loyalty and generate positive word-of-mouth, which is invaluable for your business's growth.

Lastly, embrace the power of continuous learning and adaptation. The online business landscape is constantly evolving, and staying ahead of the curve is essential. Stay abreast of industry trends, invest in your personal and professional growth, and adapt your business strategies accordingly. Embrace failures as learning opportunities and continuously refine your approach to achieve sustained success.

Starting and growing a successful online business requires dedication, perseverance, and a deep understanding of your target audience. By following these principles and leveraging the power of the internet, millennials can unlock their true potential and achieve financial success in the digital age.

Chapter 5: Navigating the Job Market and Career Advancement

Building a Strong Resume and Cover Letter

In today's competitive job market, having a strong resume and cover letter is essential for millennials who are striving for financial success. Your resume and cover letter are the first impression you make on potential employers, and they play a crucial role in determining whether you get an interview or not. This subchapter will guide you through the process of creating a standout resume and cover letter that will help you stand out from the crowd.

Your resume should be concise, well-organized, and tailored to the specific job you are applying for. Start with a strong objective statement that highlights your career goals and what you bring to the table. List your education, relevant coursework, internships, and any certifications or additional training you have completed. Be sure to quantify your achievements and use action verbs to describe your responsibilities and accomplishments. Additionally, include any volunteer work, extracurricular activities, or leadership roles you have held to demonstrate your well-roundedness and commitment.

When it comes to your cover letter, it should complement your resume and provide additional insight into your skills and experiences. Start with a personalized greeting, addressing the hiring manager by name if possible. Use the opening paragraph to grab their attention and explain why you are interested in the position. In the body paragraphs, highlght specific experiences and skills that make you an ideal candidate for the role. Use examples to demonstrate your abilities and show how you can contribute to the company's success. Finally, conclude your letter by expressing your enthusiasm for the opportunity and providing your contact information.

Remember, the key to a strong resume and cover letter is customization. Tailor your documents for each job application, highlighting the skills and experiences that are most relevant to the position. Use keywords from the job description to optimize your chances of getting noticed by applicant tracking systems. Proofread your documents carefully for grammar and spelling errors, and consider asking a trusted friend or mentor to review them as well.

By following the guidelines in this subchapter, you will be well on your way to creating a compelling resume and cover letter that will help you secure interviews and ultimately achieve financial success in your chosen career path.

Mastering the Art of Job Interviews

In today's competitive job market, the art of acing a job interview has become crucial for millennials seeking financial success. It's not just about having a polished resume or a stellar academic record; it's about presenting yourself confidently and effectively to potential employers. Whether you're a recent graduate or a young professional looking to climb the corporate ladder, mastering the art of job interviews is essential for achieving your financial goals.

This subchapter of "Millennial Money Mastery: The Ultimate Guide to Financial Success" delves into the strategies and techniques that will help millennials excel in job interviews. It provides valuable insights and practical tips to navigate the interview process with confidence and finesse.

The subchapter begins by highlighting the importance of thorough research and preparation. It guides millennials on how to research the company, industry, and position they are applying for, enabling them to tailor their interview responses accordingly. It also emphasizes the significance of practicing common interview questions and developing compelling answers that showcase their skills and experiences.

Moreover, the subchapter explores the power of storytelling during job interviews. Millennials are encouraged to craft compelling narratives that highlight their accomplishments, challenges they have overcome, and lessons they have learned. By sharing these stories, they can demonstrate their unique value and leave a lasting impression on interviewers.

Furthermore, the subchapter delves into the non-verbal aspects of job interviews. It discusses the importance of body language, dressing professionally, and maintaining eye contact to convey confidence and professionalism. It also provides practical tips on how to make a positive first impression and establish rapport with interviewers.

Lastly, the subchapter addresses the significance of follow-up actions after the interview. Millennials are advised on how to send thoughtful thank-you notes and follow-up emails to express gratitude and reiterate their interest in the position. These gestures not only showcase professionalism but also keep their candidacy fresh in the minds of potential employers.

By mastering the art of job interviews, millennials can increase their chances of securing lucrative job opportunities and advancing their careers. This subchapter equips them with the necessary skills and knowledge to navigate the interview process successfully, ultimately leading to financial success.

Negotiating Salaries and Benefits

In today's competitive job market, negotiating salaries and benefits is a crucial skill that every millennial should master. As a millennial, you have unique financial goals and aspirations, and by effectively negotiating your compensation package, you can set yourself up for long-term financial success. This subchapter of "Millennial Money Mastery: The Ultimate Guide to Financial Success" will equip you with the strategies and tools to confidently navigate the negotiation process.

Understanding your worth is the first step to successful salary negotiation. Research industry standards, salaries for similar positions, and the cost of living in your area. Armed with this information, you'll have a solid foundation to negotiate a fair and competitive salary.

When it comes to negotiating, remember that it's not just about the base salary. Benefits play a significant role in your overall compensation package. Consider healthcare, retirement plans, vacation time, flexible work arrangements, and professional development opportunities. Prioritize what matters most to you and be prepared to negotiate on multiple fronts.

Effective negotiation requires a combination of preparation, confidence, and communication skills. Practice your pitch, anticipate potential objections, and be ready to justify your requests with concrete examples of your achievements and contributions. Consider seeking advice from mentors or career coaches who can provide guidance on negotiation tactics specific to your industry.

Timing is also crucial when negotiating salaries and benefits. Aim to discuss compensation after receiving a job offer but before accepting it. This timing demonstrates your interest in the position and allows you to leverage the offer as leverage in negotiations. Remember, negotiating doesn't mean being confrontational; it's a collaborative process to reach a mutually beneficial agreement.

Additionally, keep in mind that negotiation is not a one-time event. As you progress in your career, regularly reassess your compensation and benefits to ensure they align with your growing responsibilities and market value. Don't be afraid to advocate for yourself and ask for raises or additional perks when appropriate.

In conclusion, mastering the art of negotiating salaries and benefits is essential for millennials seeking financial success. By understanding your worth, researching industry standards, and effectively communicating your value, you can position yourself for a more rewarding compensation package. Remember, negotiation is a skill that can be learned and improved with practice, so don't shy away from advocating for what you deserve. With the strategies outlined in this subchapter, you'll be well on your way to achieving your financial goals and securing your future.

Climbing the Corporate Ladder

Climbing the Corporate Ladder: Reaching New Heights in Your Career

In today's fast-paced and competitive world, climbing the corporate ladder is a crucial aspect of achieving financial success. As millennials, we are equipped with unique skills and perspectives that can help us thrive in the business world. This subchapter of "Millennial Money Mastery: The Ultimate Guide to Financial Success" aims to provide you with the tools and strategies necessary to reach new heights in your career.

1. Building a strong foundation: The first step to climbing the corporate ladder is to establish a solid foundation. This includes acquiring the necessary education and skills, developing a strong work ethic, and building a professional network. We will delve into the importance of continuous learning, the value of internships and apprenticeships, and how to leverage your network effectively.

2. Setting clear career goals: To climb the corporate ladder successfully, it is crucial to set clear and achievable career goals. We will guide you through the process of defining your long-term vision and breaking it down into actionable steps. Our tips and exercises will help you create a roadmap for your career, ensuring that you stay focused and motivated along the way.

3. Becoming a standout employee: In today's competitive job market, being average is not enough. We will explore strategies that can help you become a standout employee, including developing strong communication skills, demonstrating leadership qualities, and cultivating a growth mindset. By going above and beyond expectations, you will position yourself as a valuable asset within your organization.

4. Navigating office politics: Climbing the corporate ladder often involves navigating office politics. We will offer practical advice on how to handle workplace dynamics, build positive relationships with colleagues and superiors, and effectively manage conflicts. Understanding the unwritten rules of the corporate world can significantly impact your career progression.

5. Seizing opportunities for growth: To climb the corporate ladder, it is essential to seize opportunities for growth and advancement. We will discuss the importance of taking on new challenges, volunteering for high-visibility projects, and seeking mentorship from experienced professionals. By continuously expanding your skillset and demonstrating a willingness to learn, you will position yourself for promotions and career advancements.

6. Balancing work and personal life: Climbing the corporate ladder can be demanding, but it is essential to maintain a healthy work-life balance. We will explore strategies for managing stress, prioritizing self-care, and fostering personal relationships. Achieving financial success should not come at the expense of your mental and physical well-being.

By following the insights and advice in this subchapter, you will be well-equipped to climb the corporate ladder and achieve financial success. Whether you are just starting your career or looking to accelerate your progression, "Millennial Money Mastery: The Ultimate Guide to Financial Success" will be your go-to resource for navigating the exciting and challenging world of corporate success.

Entrepreneurship and Freelancing for Millennials

In today's rapidly changing world, the traditional career path of working for a single employer is becoming less appealing to millennials. With a desire for flexibility, independence, and the opportunity to pursue their passions, many millennials are turning to entrepreneurship and freelancing as a means to achieve financial success. This subchapter explores the benefits, challenges, and tips for millennials looking to thrive in the world of entrepreneurship and freelancing.

One of the key advantages of entrepreneurship and freelancing is the ability to create your own destiny. As a millennial, you have grown up in the age of technology and have witnessed the rise of successful startups and self-made entrepreneurs. This has inspired you to take control of your career and create a business or freelance career that aligns with your personal goals and values.

However, it is important to acknowledge the challenges that come with this path. Entrepreneurship and freelancing require a strong work ethic, self-discipline, and perseverance. Unlike a traditional job, you do not have the security of a steady paycheck or benefits. Instead, you must be proactive in finding clients or customers, managing your finances, and continuously developing your skills.

To succeed as an entrepreneur or freelancer, it is crucial to have a clear vision and strategy. This subchapter provides practical tips on how to identify your passions and strengths, research market opportunities, and develop a business or freelance plan that sets you up for success. You will learn about the importance of building a strong personal brand, networking, and leveraging social media to attract clients or customers.

Additionally, this subchapter addresses the financial aspects of entrepreneurship and freelancing. It provides insights on managing your finances, creating a budget, and saving for the future. It also discusses the importance of diversifying your income streams and investing in yourself and your business.

Ultimately, this subchapter aims to empower millennials to embrace the opportunities that entrepreneurship and freelancing offer. By combining your unique skills, passions, and the tools available in the digital age, you can create a fulfilling and financially successful career. Whether you dream of starting your own business or becoming a successful freelancer, this subchapter will provide you with the knowledge and guidance to navigate the world of entrepreneurship and freelancing with confidence.

Chapter 6: Mastering Personal Finance Skills

Tax Planning and Optimization

In today's fast-paced world, millennials face unique financial challenges that require a different approach to achieve financial success. One critical aspect of this journey is tax planning and optimization. The ability to navigate the complex tax system and make informed decisions can have a significant impact on your long-term financial well-being. This subchapter aims to provide millennials with a comprehensive guide to tax planning and optimization, empowering them to make strategic choices that minimize their tax burden and maximize their financial success.

Understanding the intricacies of the tax system is essential for millennials who aspire to achieve financial independence. This subchapter will delve into various tax planning strategies, including deductions and credits, retirement account contributions, and investment strategies. By leveraging these tools effectively, millennials can effectively reduce their taxable income and increase their overall wealth.

The subchapter will also explore the importance of staying informed about changes in tax laws and regulations. Given the evolving nature of taxation, it is crucial for millennials to keep up-to-date with any amendments that may impact their financial planning. This subchapter will provide resources and tips for staying informed, ensuring that millennials are equipped with the knowledge necessary to make informed decisions.

Moreover, this subchapter will discuss the role of technology in tax planning and optimization. Millennials, known for their technological prowess, can leverage various digital tools and platforms to streamline their tax processes, track expenses, and maximize deductions. Embracing technology can simplify tax planning, ensuring accuracy and efficiency while minimizing the risk of errors or missed opportunities.

Throughout this subchapter, practical case studies and real-life examples will be included to illustrate the benefits of tax planning and optimization strategies. By showcasing how other millennials have achieved financial success through effective tax planning, readers will be inspired and motivated to take charge of their own financial futures.

In conclusion, tax planning and optimization are crucial components of achieving financial success for millennials. By understanding the tax system, staying informed, leveraging technology, and implementing effective strategies, millennials can reduce their tax burden and maximize their wealth accumulation. This subchapter aims to provide millennials with the ultimate guide to tax planning and optimization, equipping them with the tools and knowledge necessary to navigate the complexities of taxation and achieve their financial goals.

Insurance: Protecting Your Financial Future

In today's uncertain world, insurance plays a crucial role in safeguarding your financial future. As millennials, we are often focused on building our careers, paying off student loans, and achieving financial independence. However, one aspect that is often overlooked is protecting our hard-earned money and investments. This is where insurance comes into play.

Insurance is a contract between you and an insurance company that provides financial protection against unforeseen events or risks. It acts as a safety net, ensuring that you are not left financially devastated in the face of unexpected circumstances. By understanding the different types of insurance and their significance, you can make informed decisions to secure your financial well-being.

Health insurance is one of the most important types of insurance for millennials. It provides coverage for medical expenses, ensuring that you can access quality healthcare without the burden of exorbitant bills. With rising healthcare costs, having health insurance is not just a wise financial decision, but also a way to ensure your physical well-being.

Another crucial type of insurance is life insurance. While it may seem morbid to think about, life insurance is essential, especially if you have dependents or loved ones who rely on your income. It provides a financial safety net in the event of your untimely demise, ensuring that your family is not burdened with financial hardships.

Homeowner's or renter's insurance is also vital for millennials who have moved out or own a property. This insurance protects your belongings and property against theft, damage, or natural disasters. It provides peace of mind, knowing that you are protected against unexpected events that could otherwise lead to significant financial losses.

Additionally, it is important to consider disability insurance. This type of insurance ensures that you have an income stream if you become unable to work due to a disability or illness. It acts as a replacement for your lost income, allowing you to maintain your standard of living and meet your financial obligations.

By having the right insurance coverage, you are protecting your financial future and ensuring that your hard-earned money is not wiped out by unforeseen events. While insurance may seem like an additional expense, it is an investment in your peace of mind and financial security.

As millennials, we have the advantage of technology and access to information at our fingertips. Utilize online resources and comparison tools to research and find the best insurance policies that fit your needs and budget. Remember to review your insurance coverage periodically to ensure it is up to date and aligned with your changing circumstances.

In conclusion, insurance is a vital component of financial success. By understanding the different types of insurance and their significance, you can make informed decisions to protect your financial future. Take the necessary steps today to secure your financial well-being and enjoy the peace of mind that comes with knowing you are prepared for whatever life throws your way.

Estate Planning and Wealth Transfer

As millennials, we often find ourselves caught up in the fast-paced world of technology, social media, and career advancement. While we may be focused on building our wealth and achieving financial success, it's crucial that we also consider the long-term management of our assets. Estate planning and wealth transfer are two essential components that cannot be overlooked if we want to secure our financial future and leave a lasting legacy for our loved ones.

Estate planning involves creating a comprehensive plan for the distribution of our assets after we pass away. It not only ensures that our wishes are carried out but also minimizes tax implications and legal complications for our beneficiaries. Many millennials may think estate planning is only for the wealthy or older generations, but the truth is that everyone should have a plan in place, regardless of their financial situation.

One important aspect of estate planning is creating a will. This legal document outlines how you want your assets to be distributed, who will be in charge of managing your estate, and who will be the guardian of any minor children. Without a will, the courts will decide how your assets are divided, which may not align with your wishes.

Another crucial element of estate planning is establishing a trust. A trust allows you to maintain control over your assets even after you pass away, ensuring they are managed and distributed according to your instructions. Trusts can also provide protection against creditors and minimize estate taxes.

In addition to estate planning, millennials should also consider the various wealth transfer strategies available to preserve their hard-earned assets. These strategies can include gifting, setting up life insurance policies, or utilizing tax-efficient investment vehicles. By understanding these strategies and working with financial professionals, millennials can maximize the value of their wealth and ensure a smooth transfer to future generations.

It's important for millennials to start planning for the future early on, even if they feel like they have plenty of time. Life is unpredictable, and having a solid estate plan in place provides peace of mind and security. By taking the time to educate ourselves about estate planning and wealth transfer, we can set ourselves up for financial success and leave a lasting legacy for our loved ones.

In "Millennial Money Mastery: The Ultimate Guide to Financial Success," we delve deeper into the world of estate planning and wealth transfer, providing practical tips, expert advice, and real-life examples to help millennials navigate this often-overlooked aspect of financial planning. Whether you're just starting your career or well on your way to building wealth, this subchapter will equip you with the knowledge and tools to secure your financial future and ensure a smooth transfer of assets. Don't wait until it's too late – start planning today!

Retirement Planning for Millennials

In today's fast-paced and ever-changing world, it's easy for millennials to overlook the importance of retirement planning. With so many immediate financial responsibilities and the constant barrage of information and distractions, thinking about retirement might seem like a distant concern. However, it is crucial for millennials to start planning for their retirement as early as possible to secure a financially stable and comfortable future.

One of the primary reasons retirement planning is essential for millennials is the uncertainty surrounding social security benefits. With the rising cost of living and an aging population, it's uncertain whether social security will be enough to sustain retirees in the future. Therefore, millennials must take charge of their financial destinies and plan for retirement independently.

The first step in retirement planning for millennials is setting goals. Determine how much money you will need to maintain your desired lifestyle during retirement. Consider factors such as healthcare expenses, inflation, and potential travel or leisure activities. By having a clear picture of your retirement goals, you can then create a realistic plan to achieve them.

Next, it's crucial to start saving as early as possible. Take advantage of employer-sponsored retirement plans, such as 401(k)s, and contribute the maximum amount allowed. If your employer matches your contributions, it's essentially free money that you can't afford to miss out on. Additionally, consider opening an Individual Retirement Account (IRA) or a Roth IRA, which offer tax advantages and can further boost your retirement savings.

Another essential aspect of retirement planning for millennials is investing wisely. While it's natural to be wary of the stock market due to its volatility, investing early can significantly impact your retirement savings. Consider diversifying your investment portfolio by including a mix of stocks, bonds, and other investment vehicles. Research and educate yourself on investment strategies that align with your risk tolerance and long-term goals.

Lastly, don't forget to regularly review and adjust your retirement plan. As life circumstances change, your retirement goals and financial situation may evolve. Review your plan yearly and make necessary adjustments to ensure you stay on track.

Retirement planning may not be the most exciting topic for millennials, but it is essential for securing a financially successful future. By setting goals, saving early, investing wisely, and regularly reviewing your plan, you can take control of your financial destiny and enjoy a comfortable retirement. Don't wait until it's too late – start planning for your retirement today!

Charitable Giving and Philanthropy

In this subchapter, we will delve into the world of charitable giving and philanthropy, exploring how millennials can make a positive impact on society while achieving financial success. As a generation that values social responsibility and making a difference, millennials have the potential to shape the future through their philanthropic endeavors.

Charitable giving is not just about donating money; it is a mindset and a way of life. It involves using your resources, whether financial or otherwise, to support causes that align with your values and passions. As millennials, we have unique opportunities to leverage technology and social media to amplify our giving efforts and create a ripple effect of change.

One important aspect of charitable giving is finding a cause that resonates with you. Whether it's environmental conservation, education, healthcare, or any other social issue, take the time to research and identify organizations that are making a difference in that area. Look for transparency and accountability in their operations, ensuring that your contributions will have a tangible impact.

Financial success and philanthropy can go hand in hand. As you build your wealth, consider incorporating charitable giving as part of your financial plan. This may involve setting aside a percentage of your income or creating a separate budget for charitable contributions. By doing so, you can make a meaningful difference while still achieving your personal financial goals.

Additionally, consider the power of volunteering your time and skills. Many organizations rely on dedicated volunteers to support their missions. By donating your time, you can make a direct impact on the ground and gain valuable experiences that can enhance your personal and professional growth.

Furthermore, don't underestimate the power of collective action. Join forces with other like-minded individuals or start a giving circle to pool resources and maximize your impact. By collaborating and combining your efforts, you can create a more significant change than you could achieve alone.

Lastly, remember that philanthropy is not limited to monetary donations. You can also use your voice to raise awareness about important causes, advocate for change, or support grassroots movements. Social media platforms provide a powerful tool to amplify your message and inspire others to take action.

In conclusion, charitable giving and philanthropy are essential components of financial success for millennials. By aligning your values with your financial goals, you can make a positive impact on society while achieving personal fulfillment. Whether through financial contributions, volunteering, or advocacy, embrace the power you have to create change and leave a lasting legacy.

Chapter 7: Overcoming Financial Challenges and Pitfalls

Dealing with Financial Stress and Anxiety

Financial stress and anxiety are common among millennials as they navigate the complex world of money management. However, it is crucial to understand that these challenges can be overcome with the right strategies and mindset. In this subchapter, we will explore effective ways to deal with financial stress and anxiety, empowering millennials to achieve financial success.

1. Identify the Source of Stress: The first step in dealing with financial stress is understanding its root cause. It could be overwhelming debt, lack of savings, or uncertainty about the future. By pinpointing the specific areas causing anxiety, millennials can develop targeted solutions.

2. Create a Realistic Budget: A well-planned budget is essential for financial success. Start by tracking expenses and income, and then allocate funds to cover essential needs, savings, and debt repayments. Having a clear budget helps millennials regain control over their finances and reduces anxiety.

3. Develop an Emergency Fund: Building an emergency fund acts as a safety net during unexpected situations, such as job loss or medical emergencies. Setting aside a portion of income each month will gradually strengthen this fund, providing peace of mind and reducing financial stress.

4. Seek Professional Advice: If financial stress seems overwhelming or complex, consider seeking guidance from a financial advisor. They can provide personalized strategies to manage debt, invest wisely, and set achievable

financial goals. Having an expert on your side can alleviate anxiety and provide clarity.

5. Focus on Financial Education: Educating oneself about personal finance is crucial for long-term financial success. By learning about budgeting, saving, investing, and managing debt, millennials can make informed decisions and reduce financial stress. Many online resources, books, and podcasts cater specifically to millennials seeking financial knowledge.

6. Practice Self-Care: Managing financial stress requires mental and emotional well-being. Engaging in activities that promote self-care, such as exercise, meditation, hobbies, and spending quality time with loved ones, can help reduce anxiety and improve overall financial well-being.

7. Celebrate Small Wins: Celebrating small financial victories, such as paying off a debt or achieving a savings goal, is vital for maintaining motivation and reducing stress. Recognize and reward yourself for progress made on the journey to financial success.

By implementing these strategies, millennials can tackle financial stress and anxiety head-on, paving the way for a financially secure future. Remember, financial success is a journey, and taking small steps towards it will lead to significant results.

Avoiding Common Financial Mistakes

In today's fast-paced world, millennials are constantly bombarded with financial decisions that can make or break their future. From student loans and credit card debt to saving for retirement, it's easy to get overwhelmed and make common financial mistakes. However, with the right guidance and knowledge, millennials can navigate the complex world of finance and achieve long-term financial success. In this subchapter, we will address some of the most common financial mistakes made by millennials and provide practical tips to avoid them.

One of the biggest financial mistakes millennials often make is taking on excessive student loan debt without fully understanding the long-term consequences. It's crucial to research and compare different loan options, scholarships, and grants before committing to a specific college or university. Additionally, creating a budget and living within your means can help minimize the need for excessive borrowing.

Another common mistake is overspending on credit cards and accumulating high-interest debt. Millennials are often enticed by flashy advertisements and the allure of instant gratification. However, it's important to remember that credit cards are not free money. Learning to use credit responsibly, paying off balances in full each month, and avoiding unnecessary purchases can prevent the accumulation of debt that can take years to pay off.

Millennials also tend to neglect saving for retirement, as it seems like a distant goal. However, the power of compounding interest makes starting early crucial. By contributing even a small percentage of their income towards retirement accounts, millennials can take advantage of the time they have to grow their investments and secure a comfortable future.

Investing in oneself is another key aspect of financial success. Many millennials prioritize short-term pleasures over long-term investments in their education, skills, and personal development. By continuously learning, acquiring new skills, and seeking opportunities to grow professionally, millennials can increase their earning potential and build a solid foundation for financial success.

Lastly, failing to build an emergency fund is a common mistake that can leave millennials vulnerable to unexpected expenses or job loss. Setting aside a portion of each paycheck into an emergency fund can provide a safety net during difficult times and prevent the need to rely on credit cards or loans.

In conclusion, avoiding common financial mistakes is essential for millennials aiming for financial success. By understanding the consequences of excessive student loan debt, practicing responsible credit card usage, saving for retirement, investing in oneself, and building an emergency fund, millennials can set themselves on the path to financial security and freedom. With the right knowledge and discipline, millennials can overcome the challenges they face and achieve their financial goals.

Managing Impulse Buying and Consumerism

In today's fast-paced and consumer-driven world, managing impulse buying and consumerism has become a critical skill for millennials seeking financial success. We live in a society where advertisements are constantly bombarding us with enticing offers, making it increasingly challenging to resist the urge to make impulsive purchases. However, by understanding the pitfalls of impulse buying and adopting effective strategies, millennials can regain control over their finances and pave the way towards achieving their long-term financial goals.

Impulse buying refers to the act of purchasing items on a whim without careful consideration of their necessity or long-term impact on our finances. It is a common behavior that often results in unnecessary expenses, debt accumulation, and hindered financial growth. Recognizing the negative consequences of impulse buying is the first step towards taking control of our finances.

To combat impulse buying, it is essential to develop a mindful approach to spending. This involves creating a budget and sticking to it, prioritizing needs over wants, and adopting a "wait and think" strategy before making any non-essential purchase. By giving ourselves time to evaluate whether a purchase aligns with our long-term financial goals, we can avoid impulsive decisions that may lead to regret later on.

Additionally, understanding the tactics employed by advertisers and marketers is crucial in resisting the temptation of impulse buying. Advertisements often play on our emotions and desires, creating a false sense of urgency or exclusivity. Millennials must become savvy consumers by critically evaluating marketing messages and recognizing manipulative techniques. By doing so, we can make informed decisions based on our own needs and values rather than falling victim to the allure of impulse buying.

Consumerism, on the other hand, refers to the culture of excessive consumption driven by societal pressure and the need for instant gratification. To break free from the cycle of consumerism, millennials must shift their mindset from material possessions to experiences and personal growth. This shift in perspective allows for more conscious spending and a focus on investments that align with our long-term financial goals.

In conclusion, managing impulse buying and consumerism is an essential skill for millennials on their journey towards financial success. By adopting a mindful approach to spending, understanding marketing tactics, and shifting our focus to personal growth, we can regain control over our finances and pave the way for a more secure financial future. Remember, financial success is not about the things we own, but rather the choices we make.

Overcoming FOMO (Fear of Missing Out)

In the age of social media and constant connectivity, millennials are particularly susceptible to FOMO (Fear of Missing Out). This fear can manifest itself in various ways, such as feeling the need to constantly check social media feeds, comparing oneself to others, or making impulsive purchases to keep up with the latest trends. However, FOMO can have a detrimental effect on one's financial success and overall well-being.

In this subchapter, we will explore strategies to overcome FOMO and attain financial mastery, paving the way for long-term success. By understanding and addressing our fears, we can make deliberate decisions that align with our financial goals and values.

Firstly, it is essential to recognize the impact of FOMO on our financial health. Constantly chasing after the newest gadgets, luxury vacations, or trendy experiences can lead to unnecessary debt and financial stress. By acknowledging the negative consequences of FOMO, we can begin to shift our mindset and focus on what truly matters to us.

One effective strategy for overcoming FOMO is to practice gratitude. Rather than dwelling on what we don't have, we can cultivate a sense of appreciation for what we do have. This shift in perspective allows us to find contentment in our current circumstances and make more mindful financial choices.

Another powerful tool is setting clear financial goals. By defining our priorities and aligning our spending with these goals, we can avoid falling into the trap of impulsive buying. When faced with the temptation to spend on something that triggers FOMO, we can evaluate whether it aligns with our long-term financial vision. This deliberate decision-making process empowers us to stay focused and make choices that contribute to our financial success.

Additionally, it is important to curate our social media feeds. Unfollow accounts that trigger feelings of inadequacy or envy and instead follow accounts that inspire and educate us about financial well-being. Surrounding ourselves with positive influences can help alleviate FOMO and foster a healthier relationship with money.

Ultimately, overcoming FOMO requires self-awareness, discipline, and a commitment to financial success. By understanding the impact of FOMO on our financial health, practicing gratitude, setting clear goals, and curating our social media feeds, we can overcome the fear of missing out and embark on a journey towards financial mastery. The path may not always be easy, but the rewards of financial success and peace of mind are well worth the effort.

Recovering from Financial Setbacks

Introduction:
In our journey towards financial success, setbacks are bound to happen. Whether it's due to unforeseen circumstances, poor financial decisions, or economic downturns, the key to achieving long-term financial success lies in how we recover from these setbacks. This subchapter will provide invaluable insights and practical strategies specifically tailored to millennials, empowering them to bounce back from financial setbacks and continue on their path to financial mastery.

1.   Embrace   a   Positive   Mindset:
Recovering from financial setbacks starts with cultivating a positive mindset. Understand that setbacks are temporary and view them as learning opportunities rather than failures. By adopting a growth mindset, millennials can

proactively seek solutions, explore new opportunities, and persevere through challenges.

2. Assess the Situation: Take a step back and objectively assess your financial situation. Identify the root causes of the setback, whether it's excessive debt, job loss, or unexpected expenses. This self-reflection will help millennials create a roadmap for recovery and avoid similar mistakes in the future.

3. Create a Realistic Budget: Developing a budget is crucial during times of financial recovery. Analyze your income, expenses, and savings goals to create a realistic budget that aligns with your current financial situation. Cut unnecessary expenses, prioritize debt repayment, and allocate funds towards building an emergency fund.

4. Prioritize Debt Repayment: Recovering from financial setbacks often involves addressing accumulated debts. Prioritize paying off high-interest debts first, such as credit card balances or personal loans. Consider negotiating with creditors for lower interest rates or exploring debt consolidation options to streamline repayment.

5. Build an Emergency Fund: To protect against future setbacks, establishing an emergency fund is paramount. Aim to save three to six months' worth of living expenses in a separate savings account. Automate contributions to this fund, treating it as a non-negotiable monthly expense.

6. Seek Professional Advice: Don't hesitate to seek professional financial advice during your recovery journey. Consult a certified financial planner or counselor who specializes in helping millennials navigate

financial setbacks. They can provide personalized guidance, help you create a tailored plan, and keep you accountable.

7.   Invest   in   Personal   Development: While recovering from setbacks, invest in yourself by acquiring new skills, enhancing your education, or seeking additional certifications. This not only adds value to your resume but also increases your chances of finding better employment opportunities with higher earning potential.

Conclusion:
Recovering from financial setbacks is an integral part of the journey towards financial success. By maintaining a positive mindset, assessing the situation, and implementing practical strategies like budgeting, debt repayment, and building an emergency fund, millennials can regain control of their finances and continue on their path to financial mastery. Stay determined, seek professional guidance when needed, and remember that setbacks are temporary roadblocks on the way to achieving long-term financial success.

Chapter 8: Creating a Wealth Mindset and Long-Term Financial Success

Developing Healthy Money Habits

In a world filled with endless financial temptations and instant gratification, developing healthy money habits has become more crucial than ever for millennials. As a generation known for its unique financial challenges, it is essential for us to master the art of financial success. This subchapter aims to provide millennials with practical strategies and insights to develop healthy money habits that will set them on the path to financial freedom.

1. Understanding the Power of Budgeting: Creating a budget is the foundation of healthy money management. By tracking income and expenses, millennials can gain a clear understanding of their financial situation and make informed decisions. This subchapter will provide step-by-step guidance on how to create a realistic budget and stick to it.

2. Saving and Investing for the Future: Saving and investing are vital components of building wealth and securing financial stability. This section will introduce millennials to the various saving and investment options available, such as retirement accounts, stocks, mutual funds, and real estate. It will also offer practical tips on how to start saving and investing, even with limited resources.

3. Tackling Debt and Managing Credit: Debt can be a significant burden for millennials, hindering their financial progress. This subchapter will provide strategies for effectively managing and reducing debt, including techniques for prioritizing payments and negotiating with creditors. It will also emphasize the

importance of maintaining a good credit score and offer tips on how to do so.

4. Cultivating a Healthy Mindset: Developing healthy money habits is not just about numbers; it also requires a shift in mindset. This section will explore the psychology of money and offer strategies for overcoming limiting beliefs and adopting a positive money mindset. It will encourage millennials to view money as a tool for achieving their goals rather than a source of stress or anxiety.

5. Building Multiple Streams of Income: In today's gig economy, millennials have the opportunity to diversify their income streams and increase their earning potential. This subchapter will discuss various side hustle ideas and entrepreneurial ventures that can supplement traditional income sources. It will also provide guidance on how to turn passions and hobbies into profitable ventures.

By incorporating these strategies and insights into their daily lives, millennials can pave the way for a financially successful future. This subchapter in "Millennial Money Mastery: The Ultimate Guide to Financial Success" is designed to empower millennials with the knowledge and tools they need to develop healthy money habits and achieve their financial goals.

Practicing Mindfulness and Gratitude in Finances

In today's fast-paced and consumer-driven world, it is easy to get caught up in the never-ending cycle of chasing material possessions and constantly striving for more. As millennials, we have grown up in a time where instant gratification is the norm, and financial success is often equated with material wealth. However, true financial success goes beyond just accumulating money and possessions; it encompasses a sense of mindfulness and gratitude.

Mindfulness is the practice of being fully present in the moment, aware of our thoughts, feelings, and actions. When it comes to our finances, mindfulness allows us to make conscious decisions about our spending and saving habits. By being aware of our financial goals and values, we can align our actions with what truly matters to us. This means not mindlessly swiping our credit cards or making impulsive purchases, but rather taking the time to consider the long-term impact of our financial decisions.

Gratitude, on the other hand, is the practice of recognizing and appreciating the abundance in our lives. In the context of finances, gratitude allows us to shift our focus from what we lack to what we already have. It is about being thankful for the income we earn, the opportunities we have, and the resources available to us. By cultivating a mindset of gratitude, we can avoid the trap of constantly comparing ourselves to others and feeling the need to keep up with societal expectations.

Practicing mindfulness and gratitude in our finances can have profound effects on our overall well-being and financial success. By being mindful, we can avoid unnecessary debt, make better financial decisions, and create a more secure future for ourselves. Gratitude, on the other hand, helps us cultivate a sense of contentment and fulfillment, which can lead to a healthier relationship with money.

To incorporate mindfulness and gratitude into our financial lives, we can start by creating a budget that aligns with our values and priorities. By tracking our expenses and income, we can become more aware of our spending patterns and make adjustments where necessary. Additionally, setting aside time each day to reflect on what we are grateful for in our financial lives can help us shift our mindset and appreciate the abundance that already exists.

In conclusion, true financial success goes beyond material wealth; it involves practicing mindfulness and gratitude in our finances. As millennials, we have the opportunity to create a healthier relationship with money by being fully present in our financial decisions and appreciating the abundance that already exists in our lives. By doing so, we can achieve not only financial success but also a sense of fulfillment and contentment.

Setting Long-Term Financial Goals

In today's fast-paced world, millennials face unique challenges when it comes to achieving financial success. The constant distractions and the pressure to keep up with the latest trends can often hinder our ability to plan for the future. However, by setting long-term financial goals, we can take control of our financial destiny and pave the way for a more secure and prosperous future.

This subchapter of "Millennial Money Mastery: The Ultimate Guide to Financial Success" is dedicated to helping millennials set and achieve their long-term financial goals. Whether you dream of buying a home, starting your own business, or retiring early, this guide will provide you with the tools and strategies needed to turn your dreams into a reality.

The first step in setting long-term financial goals is to identify your aspirations. Take the time to reflect on what truly matters to you and what you hope to achieve in the future. Do you want to travel the world? Do you dream of financial independence? By pinpointing your goals, you can create a roadmap that will guide your financial decisions.

Once you have defined your long-term goals, it's crucial to break them down into smaller, more manageable milestones. This helps to maintain motivation and allows you to track your progress along the way. For example, if your goal is to buy a home in the next five years, you can set yearly savings targets or focus on improving your credit score.

Financial success is not just about saving money; it also involves investing wisely. In this subchapter, we will explore various investment opportunities and strategies suitable for millennials. From stocks and mutual funds to real estate and cryptocurrencies, we will discuss the pros and cons of each option, empowering you to make informed decisions that align with your long-term objectives.

Additionally, we will delve into the importance of budgeting and creating an emergency fund. These financial habits are essential for building a strong foundation and protecting yourself from unexpected expenses or economic downturns.

Setting long-term financial goals may seem daunting, but with the right mindset, knowledge, and tools, millennials can take charge of their financial future. In "Millennial Money Mastery: The Ultimate Guide to Financial Success," we provide practical advice, step-by-step guides, and real-life examples to inspire and empower you along your journey to financial success. Remember, your dreams are within reach – it's time to start setting long-term financial goals and turn them into a reality.

Investing in Self-Development and Continuous Learning

In today's fast-paced world, where information and technology are constantly evolving, investing in self-development and continuous learning has become more important than ever before. As millennials, we have grown up in a time of unprecedented change, where traditional career paths are being disrupted, and new opportunities are emerging.

In this subchapter of "Millennial Money Mastery: The Ultimate Guide to Financial Success," we will explore the significance of investing in ourselves and how continuous learning can pave the way to financial success.

As millennials, we are often characterized by our desire for personal and professional growth. We understand the importance of honing our skills, staying relevant, and adapting to the ever-changing market demands. Investing in self-development is not only crucial for career advancement but also for financial success.

One of the key aspects of investing in self-development is identifying our strengths and weaknesses. By understanding our unique abilities, we can focus on developing our strengths further, while also working on areas that need improvement. This self-awareness allows us to make informed decisions about our career paths and helps us align our goals with our passions.

Continuous learning is another essential component of personal and financial growth. The world is constantly evolving, and to stay ahead, we must commit ourselves to lifelong learning. This could involve pursuing higher education, attending workshops and conferences, or even taking online courses. By expanding our knowledge and skills, we increase our marketability and open doors to new opportunities.

Furthermore, investing in self-development can also lead to increased confidence and a stronger mindset. As millennials, we face unique challenges and uncertainties. By continuously learning and growing, we equip ourselves with the tools to overcome obstacles and adapt to change. This resilience is crucial for financial success, as it allows us to navigate through various market conditions and capitalize on emerging trends.

In conclusion, investing in self-development and continuous learning is vital for millennials seeking financial success. By identifying our strengths, addressing our weaknesses, and constantly expanding our knowledge, we can position ourselves for lucrative opportunities and build a secure financial future. Embracing personal growth not only enhances our professional prospects but also enriches our lives on a holistic level. So, let's commit ourselves to self-development and embark on a journey of continuous learning, for it is through this investment that we will unlock our full potential and achieve financial mastery.

Leaving a Financial Legacy for Future Generations

As millennials, we are often focused on the present - our careers, daily expenses, and immediate financial goals. However, it is crucial to think beyond our own needs and consider the concept of leaving a financial legacy for future generations. This subchapter will explore the importance of planning for the future, building generational wealth, and the steps you can take to ensure a secure financial future for your loved ones.

Building a financial legacy is not just about accumulating wealth; it is about creating a lasting impact that can benefit your family for generations to come. By planning ahead and making informed financial decisions, you can lay a strong foundation for your descendants and provide them with opportunities and financial security.

One of the first steps towards leaving a financial legacy is to develop a comprehensive estate plan. This includes creating a will, establishing trusts, and designating beneficiaries for your assets. By doing so, you ensure that your assets are distributed according to your wishes and minimize the potential for family disputes or legal complications.

Additionally, consider investing in long-term assets such as real estate or stocks. These investments have the potential to grow over time and provide a stable source of income for future generations. Educate yourself about different investment options and seek professional advice to make informed decisions that align with your financial goals.

Another crucial aspect of leaving a financial legacy is teaching your children and future generations about financial literacy. Instilling good money habits, such as saving, budgeting, and investing, from an early age can set the stage for their financial success. Encourage open conversations about money and provide guidance on how to make wise financial decisions.

Furthermore, consider the impact of philanthropy as part of your financial legacy. Charitable giving not only benefits society but also provides a sense of purpose and fulfillment for your family. Engage your loved ones in philanthropic activities and establish a family foundation or charitable trust to continue supporting causes that are meaningful to your family.

In conclusion, leaving a financial legacy for future generations is a powerful way to create a lasting impact and provide your loved ones with financial security. By planning ahead, investing wisely, educating future generations, and embracing philanthropy, you can build a strong financial foundation that will benefit your family for years to come. Start today and take the necessary steps to ensure a bright financial future for your descendants.

Conclusion: Embracing Financial Independence as a Millennial

Congratulations, millennials! You have just completed your journey through Millennial Money Mastery: The Ultimate Guide to Financial Success. Throughout this book, we have explored various strategies and concepts that can help you achieve financial independence and create a secure future for yourself. Now, as we conclude this ultimate guide, let's reflect on the importance of embracing financial independence as a millennial.

As a generation that has witnessed significant economic challenges, it is crucial for millennials to take control of their financial situation. The path to financial independence may seem daunting, but with the right knowledge and mindset, it is entirely possible. By following the principles outlined in this guide, you have laid a solid foundation for your financial success.

One of the key takeaways from this book is the significance of budgeting and saving. By tracking your expenses and setting realistic financial goals, you can ensure that you are not spending beyond your means. This will enable you to save and invest, building a strong financial base for your future.

Another vital aspect discussed in this guide is the importance of investing wisely. As millennials, you have the advantage of time on your side, allowing you to enjoy the benefits of compound interest. By educating yourself about different investment options and making informed decisions, you can grow your wealth and create the financial freedom you desire.

Additionally, this book has emphasized the value of financial education and continuous learning. The world of finance is constantly evolving, and staying updated with the latest trends and strategies is essential. By dedicating time and effort to expanding your financial knowledge, you can make better financial decisions and adapt to the ever-changing economic landscape.

Embracing financial independence as a millennial is not just about securing your own future. It also enables you to make a positive impact on society. By achieving financial success, you can contribute to charitable causes, support your family, and even pursue your passions without financial constraints.

In conclusion, this ultimate guide has provided you with the tools needed to achieve financial independence. By budgeting, saving, investing wisely, and continuously educating yourself, you can take control of your financial future. Remember, financial success is not an overnight accomplishment, but a journey that requires discipline and perseverance.

As a millennial, you have the power to break free from financial limitations and create a life of abundance and fulfillment. Embrace the principles shared in this book, and let them guide you towards the financial success you deserve. Now, go forth and conquer your financial goals with confidence!